MY DAWAH LETTER TO KUFFAR KIN

GREGORY HEARY

Initially I was just going to write a card to you letting you know my new and first-ever wife is finally moving in with me after 3 years apart since we got married. Then I figured the message I wanted to say needed extra words to be written down on a piece of paper included within the card. As I wrote that 1 paper turned into many pages sized 8.5 inches by 11 inches. I still figured I'd send the 50 or so pages in the envelope with the letter to you. It later became clear a book would be more suitable for the message I intend to convey. Then it became evident if I'm making the letter into a tiny book custom made-for the few tribal houses I'm in contact with then perhaps I could make it a real book as a type of open letter too. As historically some famous letters eventually became books due to their benefit, although their original intention was just to be a casual letter to one individual from another. If Allah wills that would be nice if it is accepted as a good deed, but it doesn't change much about the letter content though it does to some degree; like not including my wife's name. Anyways the rest of the letter is as follows, with slight fine-tuning and edits after I decided to make it into a publicly available book.

From: Gregory Heary

To: My tribal relatives

My wife and I, who got married according to Islamic Shariah law in Dubai, UAE in May 2023, have been apart in separate countries ever since due to the American government not allowing her to enter the USA as has been our destiny thus far.

Finally the USA government has granted my non-American wife permission to come to America as the super slow screening process done by both the Biden and Trump Administrations has finally concluded that our marriage is genuine and she is not a criminal of any kind according to American standards. It only took those USA immigration geniuses about 3 years to figure that out! Anyways now we are at last able to reunite in person to upgrade our marriage and are planning to have her fly to the USA soon if Allah wills it to happen. Since you also live in the USA and are biologically part of the same tribe as me it is possible we may meet all together sometime in the future.

In such a situation there are some rules the exclusively true uniquely pure monotheist religion of Islam sets as legal standards for morality regarding interactions with "family" and anyone else on earth for that matter. In the past, while raised in your midst as a anthropomorphic Catholic Christian worshipping the human Muslim prophet Jesus, and his blessed Virgin Mother, and angels, and even a mythical holy ghost, and even a fictional magical character called Santa Claus (who is given the attributes of God) instead of worshipping Allah the only true God and Creator of the Universe; I was completely ignorant of the pure good moral rules for interacting with family and humanity as our Creator requires. Thus in the ancient past many of our family interactions were sinful due to our ignorance of good and bad as well as poor cultural standards and influences. After I was blessed with guidance to Islam in 2011, I learned some of the life-saving rules and tried a bit to some extent to follow them amongst you afterwards. Since then I have learned more and developed greater respect for the laws of our Creator and hopefully have improved with extra strictness in doing what is good and avoiding and combatting what is evil based on the prophetic standards.

Ironically Christians even claim to believe in most of the Muslim prophets who are mentioned in the man-made, mistranslated history books they incorrectly call holy scripture mislabeling them as divine revelation allegedly written by humans who we don't even know the names of inspired by the mythical ghost who allegedly told dozens of different people to write such contradictory history books without consulting each other or even knowing others were writing stuff too, full of polytheistic anthropomorphism and slander of the prophets in the languages of Hebrew and Greek which none of the prophets spoke, except maybe prophets Zachariah, John and Jesus who possibly spoke Hebrew as an alternative language after Nabatean Aramaic despite Hebrew not being the language of the Muslim prophets such as Abraham/Moses/David/Solomon etc; and only being invented by the Jews after they corrupted the prophetic religion into racism.

Anyways the point of this letter is to inform you of some of the rules for interactions that we as Muslims live by that will surprisingly impact potential interactions with you based on my past experiences with you.

1. We worship the Creator of the Universe 5 times every day at specific times which change every day based on how much sunlight/moonlight the Creator decreed for there to be that day. Basically at dawn, noon, afternoon, sunset and nighttime we have to pray Salat for a few minutes and only have a limited time-frame to do so usually lasting a few hours. By missing a single prayer, for an invalid reason it is disbelief and apostasy according to the seemingly correct Scholastic opinion, such a sin must be sincerely repented from and avoided. Typically the only reasons for a Muslim to miss prayer is if they have menses, post-natal bleeding, are insane, are below the age of 10 lunar years when praying 5 times a day becomes obligatory, or are unintentionally unconscious due to accidental sleep during a prayer time, or they are in a coma. So getting together with the tribe is no reason to delay a prayer to the Creator of the Universe, even if those tribe members are

Kuffar (disbelievers) or Mushrikun (polytheists). So when we are together any meeting will be interrupted when it is time to pray and Godwilling we will pray at the beginning of the prayer time window because it is more rewarding and pleasing to God when one prays at the earliest valid time rather than delaying it a few minutes or more. So every day the Creator gives us life to worship with, our life revolves around our divinely legislated prayer schedule wherever we are in the universe created by the one we pray to.

2. Many times it has been made known that as a Muslim man I am not allowed to see or touch certain females who are not super close genetic blood relatives of the type which marriage would be illegal to, such as my mom or blood aunts or grandmothers or any non-existent sisters. The textual evidence for this position is found in the same chapter my wife's dowry book was about, Quran 24:30-31,

Tell the believing men to reduce [some] of their vision and guard their private parts. That is purer for them. Indeed, Allah is Acquainted with what they do. (30) And tell the believing women to reduce [some] of their vision and guard their private parts and not expose their adornment except that which [necessarily] appears thereof and to wrap [a portion of] their headcovers over their chests and not expose their adornment except to their husbands, their fathers, their husbands' fathers, their sons, their husbands' sons, their brothers, their brothers' sons, their sisters' sons, their women, that which their right hands possess, or those male attendants having no physical desire, or children who are not yet aware of the private aspects of women. And let them not stamp their feet to make known what they conceal of their adornment. And turn to Allah in repentance, all of you, O believers, that you might succeed. (31)

While Quran 4:23 clearly describes who I'm not allowed to marry, as cited above, so anyone not mentioned would be considered a legal stranger in which marriage with would not be incest.

" Forbidden to you (for marriage) are: your mothers, your daughters, your sisters, your father's sisters, your mother's sisters, your brother's daughters, your sister's daughters, your foster mother who gave you suck, your foster milk suckling sisters, your wives' mothers, your step daughters under your guardianship, born of your wives to whom you have gone in - but there is no sin on you if you have not gone in them (to marry their daughters), - the wives of your sons who (spring) from your own loins, and two sisters in wedlock at the same time, except for what has already passed; verily, Allah is Oft-Forgiving, Most Merciful."

As for me touching other such women, like cousins of the opposite gender, Ma'qil ibn Yasar reported: The Messenger of Allah said: *"For an iron nail to pierce the head of one of you would be better for him than to touch a woman who is not lawful for him."* Mu'jam al-Kabīr lil-Ṭabarānī 20/211 Grade: Sahih

Whereas this rule of not looking or touching the opposite gender for marriable strangers applies both ways for men and women. So likewise my wife is not allowed to touch any guys who in some possible scenario at some possible date it could possibly be lawful for her to marry. So up to this point in time the only two guys in our specific tribe my wife can theoretically have any physical contact with is myself and my dad because it forbidden to marry your husband's father so he is technically a sort of guardianship relative of hers now due to my marriage to her. Thus my message to every guy in our tribe is: "*If you aren't me or my dad, keep your hands to yourself and off my wife!*" Don't try to give her no hugs, or handshakes, or fist bumps, or a pat on the back or nothing. As adults we can just talk politely courteously without any physical contact with the opposite genders. For those boys under the age of puberty there is an allowance if they don't yet understand the difference between males and females yet. But if they know the difference between a boy and girl then they know enough to not touch someone else's wife. What about the girls in our tribe? I know you are all extra friendly with the physical contact attempts despite hating our God and our religion and ourselves due to our God and religion, and despite me trying to duck out of any unlawful contact no matter how many times we notify you of our position of it. Surely girl on girl contact is okay? Well ordinarily as long as it's not lesbianesque in nature one can think it could be okay, however I believe in a classical safer understanding of the Quran verse where Allah forbids showing affection to disbelievers as explained in 58:20-22,

> *"Indeed, the ones who oppose Allāh and His Messenger - those will be among the most humbled. Allāh has written [i.e., decreed], "I will surely overcome, I and My messengers." Indeed, Allāh is Powerful and Exalted in Might. <u>You will not find a people who believe in Allāh and the Last Day having **affection** for those who oppose Allāh and His Messenger</u>, even if they were their fathers or their sons or their brothers or their kindred. Those - He has decreed within their hearts faith and supported them with Ruh(proofs and true guidance) from Him. And We will admit them to gardens beneath which rivers flow, wherein they abide eternally. Allāh is pleased with them, and they are pleased with Him - those are the party of Allāh. Unquestionably, the party of Allāh - they are the successful.*

So personally I sincerely firmly believe "affection" can be defined as behavior which includes hugs/kisses. Surely you will agree a hug or a kiss is a type of showing affection/love.

Whereas I have written extensively on the topic of love for God and the prophets of God making love for any disbeliever in Allah and his prophets impossible to exist in a believer's heart, as well as the lack of words available in the English language to appropriately express what is in a Muslim's heart for non-Muslim tribal members. I would explain it briefly as such: *"As Muslims there are many different emotions in the heart for non-Muslim tribal members."*

1. There is divinely obligated hatred of disbelief and disbelievers as well as divinely obligated hatred for sins and sinners even if those sinners were Muslim family members. Sinners are to be hated due to their publicly known sins that are not known to have been repented from. Therefore generally I hate every sinner, Muslim or Kafir except those who I have a prophetically sourced textual evidence that Allah is pleased with them and has forgiven their sins making hatred of that elite category a great transgression against Allah. Hatred for those in that category implies Allah is pleased with people and you are displeased with them thus making such hatred amount to very

dangerous attitudes towards God. Some members in this special blessed category include:

- all the prophets
- all the angels(who are sinless anyways and have no freewill to sin),
- certain non-prophet Muslims throughout history like the Virgin mother of Jesus, or the Muslim wife of Pharaoh who persuaded Pharaoh to raise Moses as a child who Pharaoh later executed due to her belief in Moses and his religion, the magicians who Moses defeated and who then repented believing in Islam prior to Pharaoh butchering them.
- The Sahabah(contemporary Muslim companions of prophet Muhammad)
- A very tiny number of people whom the prophet mentioned by name who were not Sahabah, some of whom he did not meet though they lived in his lifetime and some who would exist in the future. Such as the future companions of the Muslim Prophet Jesus, who will return for his only 2nd reappearance on earth to deal the final death blow to the dying Christian lies they call a faith, and fight against the antichrist who is a 100% human doing high-level magic and

claims to be God. These Muslims will join Jesus and the Mahdi(prophesied 100% human very kind competent and just Muslim ruler of that area at that time) when Jesus returns to earth from Paradise descending at the white minaret at one of the mosques in Damascus, Syria. Whereupon Prophet Jesus will then inform certain Muslims of that army of their rank in paradise while they are still alive. Though we don't know them yet it is forbidden to hate such people prophesied to exist in the future.

Such humans who may sin but are guaranteed paradise whether already dead or yet to be born, and I may have forgotten some categories accidentally, are all creatures who it is sinful and dangerous to hate, making them the exception to the rule which obligates hating every sinner according to their level of known sinfulness.

As we all know none of you are on that special list at this time. Neither are me or my wife. So religiously it is a part of Islam to hate myself according to my known level of sinfulness, and my wife according to her known level of sinfulness and each and every one of you accordingly. And disbelief in Islam is a huge sin that really tips the scale. Whereas my love for myself and my love for my wife as Muslims whom Allah loves for their goodness despite hating their sinfulness simultaneously, does not apply to any of you because Allah does not love non-Muslims and that's why when they die they get punished eternally by special powerful harsh Angels of Allah who do not tire and do not feel pity and do not take bribes who punish disbelievers and even sinful Muslims temporarily whether in the grave, or the yet to come Day of Judgement, or the scorching Hellfire itself without mercy or intercessor or chance to return to life and make changes they wish they could make.

Yet despite love for non-Muslims being nonexistent and sinful, there are some positive emotions in the heart that are lawful, natural and even extremely difficult to vanish from most humans. Such positive emotions I do feel for you as tribal members despite your known disbelief in the true religion of Islam. They include things that can be described with words like: *"Natural caring affinity or fondness due to belonging to the same human race and same biological tribal tree."* Despite religious differences, tribal kinship is a merciful type of bond that Allah typically creates within human hearts for the benefit and stability of society amongst both Muslims and non-Muslims alike. This type of natural bond is part of Allah's mercy for the creation and is comparable to the mercy animals have for those of the same species or family. Such as a deer lifting her hoof to allow her child to drink milk is just one part of 1% of the vast mercy Allah has spread throughout the Universe amongst creatures, while saving the rest of the 99% of his mercy to forgive those who sincerely believe in and practice his exclusive perfect faith of Islam. Thus it is also disbelief in Allah's mercy to deny the bond we share as humans; and humans that have much closer connections to each other than work relationships or teammates. As special biological tribal bonds exist amongst most of us, though some may be just in-laws related by marriage, these ties must be respected and honored given their appropriate importance in life as Allah orders.

Sadly I have struggled immensely with this part of Islam and admittedly have mightily failed in being as good of a relative as Islam says I should be.

Many excuses can be made such as distance and time, etc. But mainly I am more of a writer than a talker, and I get anxious in social settings because it is extremely risky to communicate verbally because it is so reactionary and unpredictable that causes many sinful words and sinful experiences to occur that will be harmful in both this life and the next life. So I am ill-equipped for talking verbally because it is such a huge responsibility that no sane person who believes in the Day of Judgement would enjoy talking even if they could confidently predict their speech in advance in its entirety. Because even if you speak what is good or remain silent as Prophet Muhammad taught us, then at the end of your life you still will have to answer to the Creator of your tongue as to why you said each syllable you uttered once you became of the age of spiritual accountability when it is possible to be sinful. So simply put, I am not a good verbal communicator and fear it strongly. Thus when you factor that into an equation where we have entirely conflicting religions and lifestyles with very few similarities despite those close important tribal ties, then it's extremely difficult for me to perfectly be the good relative I am divinely ordered to be while at the same time not compromising my religion which you know very very very little about and don't care much to accommodate or even discuss our differences in religion. So it's easier to balance on the deadly high elevation tightrope walk in a circus act than balance all the facets and nuances of a healthy enjoyable tribal relationship when I'm the only Muslim in the family, now joined by my wife. Frankly speaking a theoretically English speaking alien species from another planet may have an easier time getting along where everyone is content than you and me and that's not including the rest of our tribe being involved in any meeting. The more people involved the more potential disasters and misunderstandings and mistakes and mishaps that can all turn into huge sinful and painful experiences that then make being a good Muslim member of the non-Muslim majority tribe an even harder task in the future. So with our family's level of irreligiosity and de-sensitivity to sin it's like working with radioactive explosives from my perspective. By writing this letter I am literally attempting to diffuse all the possible explosions that could hypothetically occur when an amateur is dealing with unstable radioactive explosive materials.

Hence I proceed cautiously although it is devastatingly time-consuming to write/edit this message which some probably don't have the patience or maturity to read because they don't care enough about me or my wife to do so despite them saying they love us etc.

So to be clear I hate all of you, and my wife, and myself and if Allah gives me kids I will hate them too based on their individually earned sinfulness, of which the popular "Original Sin" doctrine is a myth and babies are all born with a clean slate. Though we are not all equal nor given equal blessings or opportunities by Allah. As any honest person will recognize even if they were brainwashed to believe in the American satanic philosophy of Equality for all. Despite the crucially necessary hatred that exists for all non-Muslims until they embrace Islam, I must acknowledge the merciful bond of closeness and genuine care I have for you. Meanwhile the pure noble justice of the exclusively true prophetic faith of Islam mandates that I do not act unkindly to any of you, nor treat you unfairly, nor cheat, or deceive, or abandon, or oppress, or ignore, or boycott, or insult, or fail to be anything other than

an outstanding helper in goodness in my dealings
with you. As long as you are not an active military
combatant on a military battlefield actively using
weapons of violence against Muslims or any non-
Muslims and I am not also an active member of any
Muslim government's military actively on a
military battlefield in direct combat with you on the
other side, then Islam guarantees your physical
safety from me, your financial safety, and your
mental/emotional safety, and your reputational
safety. Meaning because of Islam not only am I
forbidden by Allah to not physically harm you, but
I cannot harm you emotionally, psychologically,
monetarily, or even reputationally even in
circumstances when you are not around to know
about it. So no gossiping, even if you all do!

And that is the kind standard of justice and mercy
that I am obligated to uphold and am striving to
maintain despite my deficiencies, all while sincerely
hating you so much I am telling you it in writing
and that I have zero love for disbelief and
disbelievers. As a famous Sahabi, Abdullah ibn
Rawahah, told the Jews of Khaibar when collecting
the Jizya tax from them so they could practice

Judaism peacefully in Khaibar despite it having
been conquered years earlier by the prophet:

> *"My hatred for you and my love for the Prophet
> will not make me act unjustly towards you."*

Thus know that, yes I hate you as you deserve
based on you yourselves individually and it
fluctuates over time as your condition and status
with Allah fluctuates and changes every second
until you die and you are finally sentenced based
on your final status. However despite this hatred
which you have chosen to receive from me due to
disbelief in Islam, Godwilling I hope to practice
good manners with you as Allah decrees which is
better than what you deserve even according to
unislamic corrupt standards of extreme entitlement.
Truly me and my wife are expected by Allah to
treat you better than you yourselves actually treat
the people upon the same false religions as you who
you claim to love and have no hatred for. Thus
proving the love of someone who doesn't love
Allah is worthless in reality and no loss to not have.

So there is no need to pretend that you love me or my wife when Allah has already said disbelievers will never love Muslims until we are disbelievers. And even if Allah destined such a wicked fate for someone, you still won't love them because they were once Muslim and your devilish hatred for Islam is so extreme. And even if anyone ever were non-Muslim from the time their parents or environment misguided them to falsehood until they die, then still you won't love them because Allah has cursed disbelievers causing enmity and disunity amongst them as a punishment for their disbelief so that perhaps they may repent before being eternally punished. So please do not lie and use the "love" word with us Muslims when we know you are insincere people who don't truly mean it. And even if you do mean it and deluded yourself into thinking you are sincere then you don't know the correct definition of the word "love" to be using it anyways because I have experienced what you proclaimed was "love" before as a Kafir from many of you. And that was love for me as a non-Muslim co-religionist. And I will tell you, though you may never be able to understand, that the hatred mixed with Islamic Justice is better and more beneficial than the "love" which you profess to have for people. Basically me hating you for the sake of Allah is better treatment from me to you than your maximum possible effort of "loving" me or my wife for the sake of whatever it is other than Allah that is causing you to allegedly "love" us. Basically with a love such as the type which you give to people, then we don't need any enemies to harm us because having "love" from people such as yourselves lost in the depths of unislamic darkness, oblivious to good/bad, right/wrong, is worse than having intelligent enemies openly trying to harm us announcing war upon us. So save your expressions of love for people who are dumb enough to be fooled or accept your false claims. From my perspective someone who doesn't love their Creator Allah by worshipping Allah alone following all his genuine prophets isn't capable of loving anything less than Allah in truth because anything else is less beneficial to them than Allah is. So if you are ungrateful to Allah and disbelieve, then you can't ever be grateful to anything less than Allah. So if you are not even capable of simple gratitude, then how can you go around saying you love someone, especially someone who you think is worshipping the wrong thing following a wrong religion and are unconvinced by their most recent prophet; Muhammad's prophethood. Most of you don't even love the devilish books called the bibles enough to read even one version of them, so you don't even love your own books of evil. Yet many falsely claim that their special dusty bible is God's holy word despite the Suhuf given to Abraham, the Torah given to Moses, the Zabur given to David and the Injeel given to Jesus being in entirely different languages and content than what the Jews and Christians constantly change, edit and differ over. Simply put I don't think you love anything even yourselves because if you truly loved yourselves you would research religions wholeheartedly and make the right choice dedicating yourself to spreading the truth, as I hope to have done, for the sake of saving yourself from the very scary eternally painful hellfire. Yet most of you think, or at least act even if you don't say it, that religious talk is taboo and it is avoided as a topic in our family gatherings as if religion itself was a deadly toxic poison that will harm us if discussed. Of which all false religions that are deviated from the truth of Islamic Salafiyyah are in one way or the other. And immature people of false religions do get dangerous when discussing religion because of the truth of their falsehood being difficult for them to handle and false religions naturally not teaching them good pure moral character or manners to handle emotional turbulence either. And that doesn't mean anything difficult to handle when discussing religion is automatically true, sometimes myths are difficult to handle as well by people who believe in rival myths. But this attitude itself of secularism is the real evil blasphemous poison recently popularized and I refuse to entertain such a devilish policy and philosophy of secularism in my life.

So we don't need to hear about your fictional love and don't need it and are not going to miss it at all. I can't forbid you from saying such stuff if you are addicted to saying such catchphrases to tribal members like me, but don't expect such slogans and catchphrases to be repeated back in return. We are members of the same tribe and got positive feelings for each other and possibly genuine care, as I am ordered by Allah to have for you which you may or may not have for me to some degree, it's as simple as that. No need to use fancy flowery words that bear no truthful meanings just because it's commonly said in such circumstances nowadays to such tribal connections.

Those very same people who would publicly claim to love me and/or my wife to our faces emphatically insisting they are truly in love with us no matter what because we are family etc, probably would have difficulty even reading this letter. Thus they truly do not love us enough to even read what we are writing to them, spending hours of our time to do so, because they may say they don't have the time, or patience, or maturity level to handle reading my letter designed to improve our relationship with each other. I didn't know that it was possible to be truly in love with something and then have a maximum character limit on how many words they can communicate to you in the hopes of improving your bond together and the future memories you can create with them. So is it really love when there is a word limit on how many words you can handle reading from the one you love? No. True love would mean not only reading such messages with focus but actually cherishing such messages to the point of benefit, rather than bitterly getting through the experience to get it over with. Some of you may even get this letter and delegate others to read it and give them the gist of it because they in reality don't care enough about me or our wife to put the time into our relationship growth. Yet despite me spending more time writing the letter than it takes to read it, the ones who refuse to read may still insist on having love for the one for whom they cannot endure reading their communications, as if reading a letter from their beloved is true painful torture. But they love the torturer who by their own admission gives them more effort than they deserve and enjoy their company? In reality such people themselves have a lot of confusion about a lot of things and say things they don't mean, and their actions of disgusted enmity betray their friendly sounding tongues. Or in some cases their "loving silence" and communication Quarantine, as I seemingly don't qualify to get any type of genuine heartfelt direct written communication from most of you in reply to my past communications. But maybe you are all just verbal communication fans? Yet even then just because I don't chat on the phone during customary phone calls made to my parents' house during sinful holiday greetings that are not recognized in the prophetic religion, most of which involve sins themselves and contribute to the decay of morality despite being dressed up as family fun or wholesome celebrations of gratitude, it doesn't mean I'm entirely unable to speak on all the other days of the year. So it's as if those same people deeply in love that may or may not read their love's letters or books for whatever reason, also do not have enough love to even directly communicate verbally through any of the advanced modern methods despite using those very same methods to communicate to non-Muslim members of the tribe who live in the very same house as me. Thus if there is equal love for all tribal members why the unequal communication amounts? Because equal love for multiple people is a myth. Noone can love anything or anyone equally even if they try to. Any who deny that are either lying or stupid. But it's okay, as I said before how I don't like verbal communication anyways. I'm just proving the double standard of contradictions where the most vocal lovers of me and my wife, not only do not love us as much as they do others in the tribe, but don't even love us enough to be courteously respectful even by their own sinful unislamic standards of respectfulness. And that's okay too, because no respect is deserved by people like me and my wife who have committed the sins we have in terms of quality and quantity. The problem is people promoting such fake love mixed with unfair injustice and insensitive careless stupidity and then getting offended at us who care about them strongly enough to explain the real feelings we have for them in depth and gentleness. They'd be feeling some kind of discomfort over our kind divinely ordained hatred and lack of love or affection due to their own personal choices of being upon what are well-known false religions that I have personally explained the falsity of in detail via my books. Now such people don't have to read my books and it doesn't matter much to me if they do or don't. Yet how can someone love another so much then spend years of non-communication, whether written or verbal, regardless of the one-way communication received by them from the other and then when in person despite such neglect and arrogant ignoring they are the ones who feel upset when their love is not believed to be true and is called out for being false and unnecessary? We Muslim tribal members admit we don't love you and have hatred for you and try with some amount of effort to treat you justly upon prophetic character. And we still feel like it is important to communicate with you regardless of the hate. Whereas you do not treat us according to the prophetic standard legislated for tribal members, but this is not expected since the disbelief in the prophetic religion is known. Yet despite the lack of justice, the denial of hatred and the fake love, the worst part is the painful lack of honesty. If you hate me and my wife due to Islam, as we know is true as Allah himself told us in the Quran, that's still okay too and is expected. So you can still hate us, and do us wrong by Islamic and unislamic standards, and even proclaim fake love for us despite our annoyance with it and exposure of its falsity. But the lack of sincere honesty with yourself is what is the worst in my evaluation of the tribal relationship ties with me and my wife. If you want to be bad to us, hate us, still say you love us in public regardless of all the above, that's not that bad for you. But please at least be real and honest with yourself inside your heart, mind and soul. You can put on a good show in front of the rest of the tribe and even change some things too to really make it seem like you are putting in effort and genuinely care. But at the end of the day/night, don't lie to yourself thinking you are the ones who love us despite our "impolite heartbreaking kind hatred" when we might actually care more about you than you do us, as could be demonstrated. It's not going to hurt us whether you are truthful to us or lie to us. Yet it will hurt you if you lie to us, but that is known and likely accepted by most of you as the cheap price to pay when punished later for the non-existent benefit in telling us lies we don't even believe. However what you probably can't handle the damage of is the far greater hurt it will cause you to lie to yourself about your fake love of us. Lying to others is one thing, and can even be fixed and repented from eventually if Allah wills despite it being a huge sin that negates true prophetic belief/faith in most cases. However how can a person who lies to themselves and believes their own lies ever fix themselves and recover from that and repent from lying to themselves? Will you apologize to yourself for lying to yourself? How can you even trust yourself again when they lied to you so many times before fooling you into believing falsehood that damaged your integrity and development? And that is the real danger and problem of this whole "I love you" lie and offense at us honestly hating you for justified religious reasons that limit us displaying affection as is customarily culturally called normal. The problem is that your soul suffers such damage from constant lying that you cannot even tell anymore when your own soul is cheating you making you trapped wandering in a fantasyland while heading towards your ultimate destiny of death and strict frightening all-encompassing supremely detailed Judgement according to very high standards of morality as is promised by Allah to every free-willed creature ever created from the human species and the jinn species. Of which both Muslims and disbelievers, and good doers and devils exist amongst both jinn and humans, and ironically those 4 categories exist amongst our human tribe as well. But I will refrain from naming any names, because I could always be mistaken or things could change as free-willed beings are always capable of doing, for better or worse.

That about covers the whole topic on the other
potential issue of us not hugging each other if we
meet and the extra detail about men not touching
most women and women not touching most men
under Islamic prophetic standards and us not
saying that we love you despite having positive
feelings while our stated hatred with Allah's help
does not come with any wrongdoing in the
slightest, lest it be sinful.

I don't think we need to say and explain our hatred
in person again in detail and it's generally impolite
to overemphasize, but it will remain until Allah
changes the conditions of either us or you. So we
don't love you, we do hate you, we can get along
peacefully with good manners and can have good
times together and we don't need to discuss that
matter any further after having clarified it in some
detail here. Unless anyone forgets then we may
have to remind you as gently as possible.
Hopefully that's a process made much easier after
you read this letter than if you didn't have this
foundational understanding of the situation of
love/hate, affection and physical contact
limitations.

3. My wife, in following the example of the
    Muslim mother of the Muslim prophet Jesus
    covers herself modestly when she is in public
    around males who are not genetic blood
    relatives, or her husband, or her husband's
    father/grandfather, or slave. So for any male
    member of my tribe, since you are neither her
    husband, her husband's father/grandfather,
    nor her slave, nor what would be considered a
    close genetic blood relative then you cannot
    lawfully see what my wife looks like
    uncovered under any circumstances.
    Additionally since we believe the stricter
    opinion of the face veil, as worn by Muslim
    women during the best and first blessed
    Muhammadean generation, and the biblical
    character of Rebekah who was the wife of the
    Muslim prophet Isaac and daughter in-law of
    the Muslim prophet Abraham, to be
    obligatory and safer for morality, then my
    wife bravely faithfully covers her face in
    addition to the standard more popular hijab
    that covers everything except the hands and
    face. Now my wife may be the first woman in

the world that you will ever meet/see
wearing the niqab covering her face in public.
And she will not remove it for you, if Allah
blesses her with spiritual steadfastness and
me with a pious looking wife. And while
there is a scholastic difference of opinion
regarding whether Muslim women can be
seen to a limited degree by non-Muslim
women, I personally follow the opinion that it
is better that Muslim women are not revealing
their bodies to disbelievers generally. Yet this
stricter opinion regarding Kafir women seeing
Muslim women is not something a husband
can legally enforce upon his wife to which
obedience in goodness is due, as he can with
Niqab in front of men. However I know that
all of you will be curious as to what my wife
looks like. Whereas if the guys cannot see
much of anything and then the girls of the
tribe can see something in private spaces
secluded from men then it is likely to lead to a
situation of gossip where the girl members of
my tribe will tell the guys what they saw
regarding my wife which the guys are not
allowed to see or know. This is a sin for

Muslims to do themselves, even moreso if disbelievers are doing it spreading Muslim secrets. Thus though I wish for my wife's body parts to remain entirely unseen by disbelieving women, I cannot prevent it islamically without my wife's 100% agreement and cooperation. However I can 100% prevent gossip about my wife's appearance especially when it involves clear sins such as a woman's body being described to a man who is not allowed to see that woman. Therefore it is a reasonable condition I can impose that any female of my tribe who ever gets to potentially see any part of my wife in private where no strange man can see, then for such females they must be sworn to total secrecy/silence and never ever tell anyone else what they have seen of what my beautiful beloved wife looks like whether they are speaking to a male or a female, Muslim or Kafir.

Hence that's an important caveat that while it doesn't need to even be explained in a Islamic environment of gender segregation or Muslim country, in America amongst modern disbelievers you are probably mind-blown at such strict rigidity regarding what the eyes can or cannot see. Despite the infamous bible portraying the human Muslim prophet Jesus as telling people to physically amputate their eyeball if it causes them to sin and the Muslim prophet Moses' famous commandments including a law not to covet another man's wife; which biblical scholars Jewish and Christian alike have explained means that men are forbidden by God to look at women they are not related or married too. In fact, the classical female Christian dress code as written by the Christian Scholars of antiquity like Origen and Tertullian themselves is actually is stricter than the Muslim dress code standards. According to the people who believed in Christianity thousands of years ago the most modest nun's outfits today are sinfully scandalous. But no self-proclaimed Christians today actually care what their leaders and Scholars in the past actually declared as good or evil, lawful or unlawful, because now American philosophical principles like freedom dictates the "pursuit of happiness" makes nearly every sin lawful and morally okay, despite God and even false religions saying otherwise. Whereas the lying preachers of

Christianity lost their military strength to impose Christian laws upon Secularist Freedom lovers. Thus most Christians joined forces with the blasphemous faith of freedom and equality since they can't beat them and are too corrupt and cowardly to fight them or flee with their faith elsewhere.

This is just like how Christians did it with the pagans prior to the Roman Emperor Constantine ordering a book be created to clarify what Christian teaching/history is in the 300s CE to unite the empire upon something, of which that book eventually after further edits and revisions until today is called the Bibles. But nobody reads those much anyways today, except Christians who become Muslims when they realize the bibles have problems and none teach what Christians have ever taught throughout all of history. Yet today as most of you are regular American Christians you likely don't even know how American philosophy changed an already corrupt Christian religion that was loosely based on multiple different bibles that were only originally compiled during the 300s to unify Christians violently fighting against each other and water down the Christian religion, by that time far distorted from the religion of the human Muslim prophet Jesus, to make it more syncretic with paganism. So thousands of years of history later, after watching thousands if not millions of hours of TV/Music/Fiction/Sports and spending maybe a handful of hours on religion a year, how much are you to blame? Maybe you remember a couple of excessively repeated common catchphrases from one of the modern versions of a special modern English bible, which preachers probably quote out of context in a church or on the internet or media elsewhere. Most of you were born and then raised and lived a life where religion is not relevant and even the most religious people amongst you is a joke in terms of religiosity according to your own faith's historical religious standards, which are not even based on prophetic standards to begin with.

It's one thing to not believe in Islam, but from my experience nobody in our tribe believes in any historical religious tradition whatsoever. You may be thinking I'm picking you apart but I'm saying you don't even have much of a traditional faith to

pick at even if I wanted to. The various individuals
belonging to different denominations, the majority
of which are some version of Christian, amongst
our tribe are pathetic when it comes to actually
practicing what they themselves claim is their
religion. The reality is all of you have syncretic
poly-religious contradicting personally independent
customized individual belief systems not based on
any actual historical individual religious leader or
textbook. Instead all of you have blended things
from various different sources of information and
then lived as easily as possible with whatever
amount of guilt your immorality allows for you to
live with without actually getting religious. Such
information sources could be a mixture from books,
movies, schools, TV, songs, plays, sports, fiction,
politics, idiots within our tribe, and other idiots
outside our tribe and some stuff is special stuff you
yourself made up all on your own which you hold
as a true smart idea that you may not even
recognize qualifies as a religious belief/principle.
Religion itself and what religion is has been
redefined many times in history by the heretics and
disbelievers causing massive confusion worldwide
that dilutes religion for even those considered

religious by today's standard. And that is across the board for both false and the truth faith of Islam. Muslims themselves also have some dilution from cultural practices and language barriers that prevent prophetic knowledge from fixing things as well as they potentially could if the people were truly sincere. Basically our tribe is full of religious extremists in the way of negligence and laziness and then I come along as a Muslim minority trying to practice the prophetic religion with firm effort. So naturally you will see me to be extreme because you are extremists yourselves in the opposite direction as us.

Hence us, as a hopefully Salafi Muslim couple, trying our best to follow genuine prophets of the Creator in modern life, in the midst of a toxic unislamic country who was only recently allowed to officially have Islam as a legal religion in the 1960s CE, despite the African slaves being Muslims, we have probably totally shocked your mind, heart and soul with our rules for moral family interactions based on the prophetic religion. Based on my past experience with our tribe typically you don't even think about religion as an actual subject unless it is a wedding, funeral, pagan/political unbiblical holiday, or when rarely going to a theatre performance called church where intoxicants are distributed in ways Christian Scholars throughout history themselves have declared sinful.

4. The next family interaction rule deals with intoxicants such as alcohol, formerly illegal in Christianity and even in America itself for years because of Christians attempting to revive some parts of classical Christianity. As well as marijuana, also now legalized in America and likely soon to be legalized in Christianity just like all drugs are technically legal according to the easily predictable Christian leaders giving in to future drug culture pressure just as they gave in to pig pressure despite the biblical prohibitions to eat pig products in both the Old and New testaments which they themselves wrote and edited. For today, most fake Christian performers will quote a possible quote from biblical Jesus loosely saying "What enters the body does not defile it, but it is what is inside the heart that corrupts the body." Thus they

knowingly falsely say pig is okay to eat, as is any food and you don't even have to eat kosher anymore either despite their own distorted version of the human Muslim Prophet Jesus and even the deviant Paul himself placing many food restrictions on the members of their faith; of which Biblical Jesus and Paul had different rules but still both agreed you can't just eat any food available. Yet pig is well-known as a no-no for Muslims and I won't write a rule for that in this letter because it is so well known as something we don't eat. Food sacrificed for, prayed upon or blessed for other than Allah is also sinfully prohibited too. Although I will say that with these food prohibitions we implement such prohibitions in our lives more strictly than you would imagine it would apply.

For instance, my wife and I with Allah's help will not go out to eat at restaurants that have the potential to be using utensils that were previously used on pig products, or non-halal meat or alcohol. We are not risking a sin to eat something off a plate, fork, spoon, knife, or cup that could have traces of sinful food/drink that may or may not have been hygienically removed to a sterilized extent that could make it lawful to use by Muslims. It's just too big of a risk and hassle to ensure the safety. Plus as a somewhat stingy person I don't even want to go to restaurants anyways even if it has totally lawful food with a music-free gender segregated section. This is because it truly is a waste of money to eat at restaurants to pay for all their cooking and handling costs when others are starving and you can save both time and money eating food not professionally cooked for you. So even if I were in the most religious restaurant in Mecca itself, I don't want to go to a restaurant because it's a wasteful industry that just contributes to world hunger and wasted time/food/labor in addition to the sins often committed in the process of a restaurant visit. In my opinion the world would be better off if most of the restaurants closed, except at high traffic tourist definitions where cooking is not practical such as airports and remote areas where food and cooking supplies are not easily obtainable for travelers etc.

But this rule is focused on intoxicants. Of which the point was, just as Christians misuse their own

books to justify any food, despite the earlier
commentators on those same books quoting other
verses to forbid those same foods, it is easy to
foresee how intoxicants with various American
legal labels today could become thought of as legal
and not sinful in the future when we interact
because of unislamic standards normalizing such
intoxicants of which I only mentioned some. The
rule for Muslims is found in the Quran verse 5:90,

> *O you who have believed, indeed, intoxicants,
> gambling, [sacrificing on] stone alters [to other
> than Allāh], and divining arrows are but
> defilement from the work of Satan, so avoid it that
> you may be successful.*

This verse also covers the prohibition on gambling
too, so I won't add gambling to the list of things we
don't do because you know now if you didn't know
already that gambling is an egregious error
according to our Creator, even if in tiny amounts
done "responsibly just for fun".

The prophet's companions asked for clarity on
intoxicants in depth because there are many
different types and new ones are often invented and
spread by evildoers. In fact, prophet Muhammad

explained the Arabic word "Khamr", used for intoxicants in the Quran, can be defined as follows; additionally citing wine as it was the most popular type of intoxicant at the time when intoxicants where abolished in all Muslim territories.

Ibn Umar reported Allah's Messenger as saying:
Every intoxicant is Khamr and every intoxicant is forbidden. He who drinks wine in this world and dies while he is addicted to it, not having repented, will not be given a drink in the (eternal) Afterlife.

Source: Sahih Muslim hadith #2003

Intoxicants are so seriously forbidden that some Muslim Scholars are even of the opinion that since it is illegal to pray any of the 5 daily prayers while intoxicated, and that because it is so difficult to get intoxicated and still pray the 5 obligatory prayers on time with sobriety, then they have ruled in certain cases consuming any intoxicant is disbelief and apostasy in Islam if it causes them to miss an obligatory prayer due to not being sober which is a condition for the validity of the prayer.

It was narrated from Ibn 'Umar that the Messenger of Allah said:

"Wine is cursed from 10 angles: The wine itself, the one who squeezes (the grapes etc), the one for whom it is squeezed, the one who sells it, the one who buys it, the one who carries it, the one to whom it is carried, the one who consumes its price, the one who drinks it and the one who pours it."

Source: Sunan Ibn Majah 3380 Grade: Hasan

Jabir reported that the Prophet said,

"Whoever has faith in Allah and the Last Day, let him not sit at a table over which wine is being served."

Source: Sunan al-Tirmidhi 2801 Grade: Hasan

Meaning intoxicants like alcohol are something so serious to us that, it's not a matter of you can enjoy it in front of us and we will just abstain and avoid it ourselves. No. We cannot interact with someone who is consuming intoxicants or have any part of the process. It is illegal to be in the same place at the same time wherever intoxicants are consumed according to the current prophetic legislation of our Muhammadean era. We could debate about the wine rules for previous generations and whether if the biblical grape juice got mistranslated as wine as society corrupted, as the prohibition era Christians in America convincingly proved, but this is not a fruitful discussion. Whether you think intoxicants are okay or not, or tolerable or not, we as Muslims are not going to be around anywhere where intoxicants are consumed. So for all the alcohol consumers, we are not going to be in the same place if you have any alcohol at all in your system. And the church wine counts as intoxicating too, so Sundays in general may be a bad day for visits if any of you are drinking that stuff during the parties they have at such places.

And such a policy furthermore tests and proves the little amount of alleged love our tribe members really have for us. For as Muslims we legally cannot be around alcohol or other intoxicants anymore than you as Americans can be around any of the drugs that America currently declares illegal weapons of mass destruction like Fentanyl. If we said we can't be at a party or event where Fentanyl is being taken, few would be angry or challenge the policy. But because of evil cultural norms where the intoxicant of alcohol, despite being one of the leading causes of death, health problems, society problems and crimes in the world, is tolerated to various extents, then someone who has zero tolerance according to prophetic standards is considered extremely strange and difficult. Whereas the really strange people are those whose mind justifies intoxicating their mind while they are in the midst of people they claim to love and enjoy the company of. And what's stranger still is not those fools, afterall they probably lost some brain cells from intoxicants, it's the members of the tribe who for years have stayed silent in the name of freedom justifying the consumption of a chemical that famously damages your brain and thinking abilities. What if any "beloved" tribe member was taking a knife inserting it in their ear trying to cut some brain cells in their head because they don't like them itching and so they say cutting the brain cells with a knife helps them feel better during a family gathering? What would you do? Would you justify their self-inflicted brain damage by saying it's legal to do in Secular Freedom loving America because they are "pursuing happiness" and they aren't forcing you to cut your own brain? Or would you take the knife out of their hand by force if persuasion didn't work? And if they were stronger to resist action and too stubborn to resist persuasion from yourself and others then wouldn't you tirelessly tell them not to harm themselves? And if they insist no matter what, then wouldn't you tell them to at least have the kindness to hurt themself when alone by themself so you are not legally held liable for witnessing the sinful stupid destructive behavior that could even harm you due to them harming more brain cells than anticipated and losing control of their mental faculties? Well that example is not even as dangerous as alcohol is because alcohol is more dangerous than cutting brain cells because it harms more than just the brain. More dangerous than any worldly harm is that alcohol damages the soul, as all intoxicants do.

So as much of a problem we have with people consuming intoxicants in our presence, under the protection of the false faith of godless freedom legalizing it, the big problem is not the attitude of the intoxicant addict. The bigger problem is the silent observer who allows such sinful public self-destruction to be done to people they claim to love and care about directly in their presence and they neither have the nerve to stop it, nor to say anything to forbid it from occurring, nor do they have moral fortitude to apply social peer pressure to limit the damage and comfortability of the sinner by removing themselves from the intoxicant consumer. Those silent devils are worse than the loudmouth intoxicated ones, because the intoxicated ones are chemically less liable and in less control of themselves than those who are sober and silent and tolerate such a serious sin that is divinely intolerable to be around for true believers and even non-islamic truthfully honest and compassionate people. Forget the tribal relationships and religion for a millisecond. If anybody is around anybody and they are a sober person who just hangs around with intoxicant consumption going on, then these cowardly sober people are not good people to be around influencing you or your family. And that is for non-tribal members being bad influences if they silently observe intoxication without objection. What about tribal members who profess love and care and affection for the intoxicated and the rest? Such hypocrisy is worse than intoxication. Such phonies can stay together and leave us alone, just as we leave alone anyone who is consuming any

intoxicant by any amount at all without considering
what any man-made law/rule is for the intoxicating
chemical consumed or the amount of it. If such
intoxicant consuming people really love us they can
interact with us while sober at events where there is
no chance for any intoxicants to be consumed. And
if they cannot stay sober long enough to have time
to interact, then they need more help than we can
provide and should not be interacting with us
because we are not qualified to provide the help
they need.

And if nobody in our tribe agrees with our policy
and sincere advisory admonition for whatever
reason that's fine, you can take your chances with
Allah's law later. But don't drag me and my wife
into an event where there are any intoxicants
because we will flee on the spot without delay nor
being polite about it as if we were fleeing from the
eternal hellfire itself. And we don't care if anyone
else supports us in this correct policy or not. Let the
freedom lovers enjoy their dumbness alone free
from us.

Semi-related to the topic of intoxicants is music. As a former Christian rapper, who published 4 albums and has a College degree in "Audio recording and production" for the field of creating music, I know a little more about music than most people. During my studies in non-islamic American college it was taught that music is an auditory drug comparable to liquid drugs, or solid drugs, or gas drugs. And music is truly more powerful than most intoxicants because most intoxicants do not come with lyrics and messages that infect your brain memories permanently sticking such information in your brain along with the buzz. Once one hit song is heard, you just memorized a sinful human's devilish message for the rest of your life to be bounced around in your brain until you die or Allah helps you forget it. While even if you do forget the damage, the ideas might have already sunk into your heart and affected your belief system about good/evil and other things. Of which most of the songs are fictional lies anyways, so it's not even like they are true stories mixed with hypnotic sounds. They are purely lies disguised. Hence the influence of music itself no matter what the song is about typically causes you to accept lies as something that's okay, because it sounds nice to hear. Think about that. When has a lie ever been something that is nice to hear? Prophet Moses forbade lying strongly as did all the prophets of Allah. But today music is often heard in public, and, as it pertains to us, at tribal gatherings. Islam forbids music as some of you may know, hence I correctly quit my music career because of being so convinced of the truth of Islam. So Muslims label music as sinful due to Quran and Hadith in general. Yet as you may have guessed my wife and I are not trying to be average typical Muslims. So generally, although some sins can be socially tolerated by us to some extent in certain circumstances, such as non-Muslim female relatives dressing in what Islam considers immodest sinful attire, music is a thing we are stricter than most on. Of which religious practicing Muslims themselves are stricter than what is considered reasonable by non-Muslims. Due to my personal experience and knowledge of music I believe it can also be classified as an intoxicant too. I believe/hope music is someday popularly categorized as a weapon of mass destruction as scientific research indicates it is, and that the music industry, I once was a part of, and sinfully addicted to myself, is shut down entirely. Of course I'm not advocating unlawful unislamic sinful violence in any way against musicians or music addicts the way politicians have gone after supposed drug dealers and how islamaphobes portray us music-hating Muslims to believe, but music is a drug or at the minimum can be classified as a soul-changing evil.

I'm just saying Music is sinful in our belief system, period. In addition, we personally believe it is more sinful than most Muslims realize or dare to say even if they do realize, because we consider it a type of intoxicant though not comparable to the chemically ingested types which make the 5 daily prayers invalid. So given my previous explanation of our position on chemically ingested intoxicants being so intolerable as to force us to leave the premises where intoxicants are being served, we personally hold a stricter position on music than the modern Muslim standard. Thus we feel to be balanced towards both chemical and non-chemical intoxicants then we should also leave any area where music is heard. However unlike with alcohol or other drugs, we can easily immediately return to a person who has been intoxicated with music because the sobriety of the music consumer returns faster than the sobriety does with other intoxicants. So in that regard music is more similar in our reactionary response to a sinful cigarette than it is to alcohol though we consider music an intoxicant and some cigarettes are not intoxicants. Cigarettes are also sinful for us to be around and known to be bad for health regardless. Although since cigarette smoking is a less popular sin in our tribe and much more easy to avoid being cross-contaminated with its harm, then we don't need to write much on cigarettes. Yet mentioning how we mildly avoid harmful cigarette smoke is useful when explaining what we do in reaction to music exposure. So we don't tolerate music, intoxicants, nor smoking harmful stinky non-intoxicants around us but each one is treated a little differently despite all being things which we dreadfully avoid like plagues.

5. As you may or may not know or have guessed, music is often found on televisions, along with highly sexualized females in unislamic dress codes and even highly sexualized males in sinful outfits and

situations too. Plus TV also contains lies and fiction which we do not tolerate even when done in jest to be funny. Which may be the hardest one of all for some tribal members. Not the TV being something me and my wife avoid being around when they are turned on, due to the potential for hearing music on it. But out of everything on this list some of you probably are going to find the not telling lies as part of your jokes to be the hardest rule of ours to comply with! This is because you are not that funny when you have to tell the truth at all times because it is sinful to tell a lie when being humorous. So due to fear of not being funny with icebreakers and laughter stifling our seriousness, you may be tempted to lie to get some laughter as background noise. Regarding lies, we know many of you lie so much when joking around that you will find it hard to control it and mistakes will happen. We will try politely reminding and advising when they do, as we hope you will do to us if and when we make mistakes. For as the famous Sahabi, Umar bin Khattab said:

As for TV, we try hard to limit our exposure as much as possible, though my parents don't cooperate much with this one. Yet since we live so far apart, and rarely see each other, I'm hoping you all can kindly pause your daily TV addiction to spend quality time and attention to us when/if we are together. Even the disrespectful sinners know it is considered rude even by today's standards to be watching TV with tribal guests around in many situations, and we are people who religiously try to avoid TV due to the intoxicant of music which is sinful in our faith even if we are personally too strict in labeling music an intoxicant. So hopefully the TV is not such a powerful idol with such complete control over you that you are unable to turn it off if we are around. If it is that powerful in your household, as it seems to be in my parents' house, then we will gladly help you with your permission and turn the TV off for you so you can better focus and enjoy our short visit. Or we can inform you of Islamic TV stations if you really need

TV amongst us. Hopefully you care more about us than the TV. Despite the TV generally having a clear advantage and domination over many of our tribe's weekly schedules in terms of quantity of time spent together. As TV shows tend to be more popular amongst many than Sunday worship services. Factually sports, movies or soap operas consume more time in our tribe's weekly schedule than the most religious of Kafir worshippers. So timewise the numbers of hours spent in your weakly faith life indicate what you really care for.

6. Vulgarities or obscenity aka swear words are also something we believe is sinful and dislike being around. Mistakes happen though and our expectations are realistic. Yet still it is worth mentioning to be aware of, and hopefully you didn't get too many sins for cussing me out due to the length of this letter and its shocking sin-bashing content.

7. I think it is well-known by now by our tribe that Muslims do not celebrate unislamic holidays like the famous ones and birthdays, anniversaries etc. Though for the record we

do have two holidays we do observe, Eid al Fitr and Eid al Adha. So it's not like we are total party poopers, but we do in effect feel it necessary to sort of rain on your parades of evil and lies regarding holiday celebrations if you are promoting them around us. If you want to do stuff like Christmas because of mistaken understandings of Jesus' birth, or even greater mistakes regarding the plot by his enemies to kill the 100% human Muslim prophet Jesus who Allah saved without him suffering any harm at all, that is your own terrible decision. But if you are expecting us to play along in any type of festivity myths and lies, or holiday related practices/traditions or events without comment then you are in for a shocking surprise. What do I mean?

The popular idol called "Santa Claus" who is worshipped by millions of children in non-Muslim countries with Christian histories is considered a literal false god given the attributes of Allah in some things like knowledge of wakefulness or consciousness and having a criteria/law of judgement regarding what is good behavior or bad behavior that gets rewarded or punished accordingly. All of you know 100% Santa Claus is a mythical fiction, and if you are young still hopefully you know now and the liars older than you are honest and caring enough to tell you. I don't recall anyone in my tribe telling me Santa Claus was not real until I doubted it in my teenage years. On the contrary many of you knowingly lied to me about Santa Claus many times for many years without feeling guilt or remorse or repenting for it. If you had sincerely repented you would wage war against Santa Claus today just as repentant drug addicts denounce drugs and discourage others from their evil. Santa Claus and other holiday myths like the Easter Bunny, Tooth Fairy, and others are often more dangerous than drugs. Because many drugs by themselves will not cause someone to burn in the hellfire for eternity. There are situations where drug induced death whether sudden or slow due to long-term damage from drugs can lead to eternal consequences of pain, but these are not sins where they are 100% unforgiveable sins that can strip a person 100% of their religious belief rendering it null and void and if died upon earns them an eternal stay in hellfire. But Santa Claus does do that. There is nobody who believes in Santa Claus who also believes in Allah and/or any version of God as depicted by any religion in the world, unless you count the cult of Santa Claus where the people only worship Santa as God.

So worshipping Santa Claus is worse to Muslims than blasphemously worshipping angels, pious people or prophets including Jesus. Of which we will also tell you and anyone who doesn't know or understand why worshipping other than the Creator, aka Shirk, is the worst most dangerous unforgiveable sin possible to commit; as such a topic comes up in the course of our communications in person or otherwise whenever it is mentioned. When evil is spoken or mentioned, the general practice upon the prophetic methodology is that we try to correct it. Whereas the worst type of the worst type of sin, called Shirk, is not doing Shirk or polytheism itself, but inviting to or promoting Shirk or polytheism/disbelief. And this is why Santa Claus though being nearly last on the list is one of the most important and dangerous things which we as Muslims are obligated to forbid. Especially when

you non-Muslims know 100% it is a total lie. It's
not like you are confused and miseducated and
heavily brainwashed about Santa Claus and his
reality like many Christians could try to say
regarding the human Muslim prophet Jesus and
why they worship Jesus instead of the Creator of
Jesus whom Jesus told us all to worship. Jesus
worship is inexcusable but Santa Claus worship is
even more inexcusable. And even the strongest
Santa lie spreaders know it is only a matter of time
before they stop preaching and let their victim
know the truth. So why lie at all? Don't you know
it's evil, sinful and damns a person to eternal hell if
they die while believing in Santa Claus? Are you so
desperate to go to hell yourself that you need the
sin of Santa Claus on your soul to get yourself a
worse spot? Because it's not just a couple years of
lying to children and then they grow up and they
know better and all is forgiven by them and they
enjoy it and you enjoy it and they survive,
disbelieve in the Santa Claus myth and happy ever
after no harm done; unless they die young and go to
hell eternally for believing in Santa. That alone is
enough for us to forbid Santa, because we care
about the kids of our tribe so they don't go to hell

due to Santa Claus if they die young. But the sin of disbelief due to Santa Claus applies to adults who teach people about Santa Claus too. We know and have established Santa Claus is a lie, and didn't even have to try to do that. We know and established with ease that Santa Claus is a false idol too who wrongly is given some exclusive attributes of Allah. Yet every sin must be repented from in this life before our death to get forgiven, or else we risk punishment for it where Allah may or may not forgive Muslims based on his own choice and their own special circumstances. Even Muslims who don't repent from sins can be punished for it in hell temporarily in a different section than non-Muslims in a less severe manner if Allah decides to torture.

Hence correct true Repentance is so important. Some conditions of a valid repentance of a sin include real regret and a sincere effort to avoid repeating the sin never to do it again. If you do commit it again then you repent again as long as it takes repeating the cycle sincerely each time trying your best 100% until the devil himself gives up and/or you grow strong enough to finally succeed in perfecting your repentance from that sin by totally avoiding it for the remainder of your life. Or you die sincerely trying. It is those Muslim repentful who can hope for forgiveness without punishment. Yet if true regret and avoidance is necessary to repent to get a chance at mercy then how does someone who lies about Santa Claus repent from that sin? Of which it is a sin of the highest level possible since it amounts to preaching idolatry, no different than if you were a Hindu preacher telling people to worship an elephant idol called Ganesh. In fact, the Hindu preacher is less sinful because he might be dumb enough to believe in the idiotic idolatry just as some Christian preachers might be dumb enough to believe in what they falsely teach about Jesus, though the majority know Christianity doesn't match the textbook they claim they get it from and even that textbook itself is not what they claim it to be even if they were silly enough to psychotically think it did. Most preachers of false religions despite doing the worst sin of the highest level possible have a better position than the preacher/teacher/supporter of Santa Claus. This is because Santa Claus teachers know 100% with no pathetic excuses or confusion or stupidity that what they are teaching is 100%

falsehood and a lie. They even admit it openly after awhile to everyone they deceive. But do they sincerely regret it and stop doing it by fighting evil?

The sad reality is that the vast majority of people who teach Santa Claus to people don't regret it. So they can't repent from it due to that. If they are in the small minority who do regret it, do they avoid doing it again with all the strength they have? No. Most of the second category double dip and continue the sinful tradition to others who are young and dumb enough to worship Satan Claus for 1 month a year. In the case of many parents, they will teach their kids until the myth dies. Then when the kids have kids of their own, both the original parents and the original victims repeat the "magical lie" again with the victims continuing the evil indoctrination of theirs to a new generation of victims. And what is the crime? The crime is disbelief in the Creator of the Universe and the exclusivity of the Creator's attributes. So it is better to give your children intoxicants than Santa Claus because that is easier for them to repent from sincerely and less risky and bad for themselves and the world, especially if they never repent from it.

Therefore because of this continuous deception of Santa Claus year after year, and death is always an unexpected moment, many people die and do not sincerely regret and stop/avoid preaching the Santa Claus religion. This means all those people who died while having not repented from teaching others about Santa Claus are doomed to eternal hellfire, except for extremely rare cases of the insane, but even that is just a hypothetical for which I myself don't know enough if insanity could be a defense for preaching Santa Claus to others as it could be for other types of disbelief in Islam and Allah or prophets. So out of everything in the world today Santa Claus is one of if not the biggest evil in the world. But with this being a family focused letter we will not turn it into an in depth expose about Santa mythology. Atheism is not as bad because even atheists could try a false excuse of being dumb and brainwashed or confused. Yet nobody except the young children Santa worshippers themselves could ever say that they actually had true heartfelt belief they were right when they believed and taught others about Santa Claus. Anyone who knows knows that 100% it's a lie. And it is a lie of idolatry they rarely ever repent from, let alone fulfill the conditions of a valid repentance where Islamic faith and practice are additional requirements.

Yet maybe you don't care and have such wicked character that you still want to have fun with the idol of Santa Claus and other such characters due to holiday fanaticism which is greater in importance than your alleged actual religious beliefs. For example, Muslims don't belief Jesus is God nor a son of God despite his lofty status as a prophet. We will say so in front of children whether you allow us to or not, agree or disagree, because it's the truth and we can prove it if you are willing to have a discussion on the topic. Maybe you don't want to discuss it and disagree and that's that. You may just try to protect your belief or your kids belief if you feel we are heretical or whatever. But many "Christians" who actually believe incorrectly about the blasphemous statements regarding Jesus' alleged godhood and sonship, while they may be bitter over us sharing our beliefs on the topic of Jesus, when it comes to Santa Claus and their kids…..

They wouldn't even let me say a word. To them it is worse for us to say their human "God" is not truthfully a god in front of their kids, than to say that the false idol of Santa Claus which they know 100% is a false lie, is not real and not coming to give their kids presents. Thus a further example of contradictions inherent in evil unislamic belief systems and lifestyles. Though the adults know Santa Claus is fake they respect the Santa Claus faith more than their own deity.

Really is speaking about Santa Claus a more sacred subject than speaking about the true Creator of the Universe? How? How can such people with such devotion to false idols they knowingly promote with certainty they are lying and fail to ever even attempt to repent from, ever have any insanely hypothetical shot at being loved by God according to any religion? They spend years and years constantly lying to the youngest members of the tribe and others directly and indirectly, intentionally and unintentionally, about idolatry until they die guarding the falsehood with more zeal and protection than they do the idolatry they actually idiotically believe in. Then upon death, people say they were good and are in a better place, not suffering at least? No! According to all traditional religions such people are disqualified from paradise.

And as Muslims we say if you are that evil and want to spread the myth of Santa Claus and go to hell forever, guaranteed as a result of that action alone, that is your decision to do. But don't stop us from speaking the truth about Santa Claus when the opportunity arises and becomes obligatory for us to do so. If such a wicked idol is mentioned in front of us at anytime of the year we must warn against it more sternly than any other violation in this letter. If you want to save the devil called Santa Claus and defend it that's your crime, but please for the sake of our Creator don't be so wicked that you hinder and forbid or outlaw the truth about Santa Claus from being told by us when the situation arises. Burn yourself in Hell forever if you want to, and the kids you teach the Santa Claus tradition too who continue it without repenting, for which you will be responsible for all who carry on the tradition after you and bear a portion of the evil results of that. Yet have mercy on us at least who are trying to tell the truth that you know is 100% true pure good factual reality. Because by fighting us for the sake of Santa Claus to the point of a total truth censorship where you prevent us from communicating the evilness of the biggest sin on earth today, then you not only are doing the biggest sin on earth today, teaching others to do it too, but you are such a devil in reality that even Satan himself cannot do much worse than what you are doing by outlawing us from saying a single letter against the worst idol on earth today. If you want to compete with Satan in your evilness then that is your choice but we are giving you advanced advice and warning of the eternal consequences of fighting against us for that choice. And our faith will not allow us to surrender to Santa Claus and it is not a battle you will win in any way even if all your most elaborate advanced strong evil plots succeed for a short while. Because Allah himself is an enemy of Santa Claus and Satan and all their promoters. And whether you believe Allah or not, the reality is ultimate victory belongs to Allah and the believers who do a good job fulfilling Allah's commands, dying in the process. So we promise you to fight against Santa Claus as long as we are guided by

Allah and blessed with life to do so. We will gladly die fighting Santa Claus so this is a war in which you would be wise to surrender and admit your error, so that perhaps you can repent and be forgiven someday if Allah blesses you with mercy. Yet even if mercy is not your destiny, you should know Santa Claus and his supporters will lose this war entirely with total humiliating defeat sooner or later. What more can I say to warn you with advice that will benefit?

Do you love Santa Claus more than me and my wife?

Do you love Santa Claus more than Allah our Creator?

Do you love Santa Claus more than whatever false deity you incorrectly worship other than Allah?

Do you love Santa Claus so much as to send others you claim to love to hellfire eternally due to your students worshipping Santa and/or preaching/teaching Santa Claus themselves at a later date without repenting?

Do you love Santa more than you love yourself and are you willing to burn in hellfire forever due to your love and protection of Santa Claus?

Well then in my opinion you are much worse than the supporters and protectors of the evil human known as the Anti-Christ. Because he at least will have some advanced high-level trickery so his preachers, worshippers, soldiers will have a better albeit invalid case to make when judged by Allah for their crimes in supporting the Anti-Christ. They have many more and better reasons for supporting the Anti-Christ than you do for supporting the idol of Santa Claus. At least the followers of the Anti-Christ can say before they are eternally punished in hell that they got tricked by his tricks. Yet Santa Claus by your own admission both privately and publicly has zero credibility or confusing tricks to deceive you into such extremely fanatical lifelong religious servitude to falsehood to the extent of waging warfare against the Muslims for Santa Claus's sake. And if such words do not motivate you to do the right thing in fighting Santa Claus too alongside us under the guidance of the correct prophetic methodology of Salafiyyah, then at least sensibly get out of the Muslims way when we are in sacred combat with the defenseless soon to be forgotten devil called Santa Claus. And know that the judgement of Allah regarding Santa Claus is even stricter than the Muslim humans position regarding him, due to our limited knowledge and analysis and argumentation abilities combined with our limited sense of evil and the ability to calculate the destructive damage Santa does as well as the greatness of Allah in how insulting it is to side against Allah for Santa Claus despite all the information and warnings Allah has destined you to receive whether you can stomach this letter and have read this far or not. Truly such hellfire dwellers who supported Santa Claus will admit that it was a deed done by them more evil than what I have described and Allah will show them the reality of the gravity of that crime as well as all the rest.

And that is what is more scary. For life is not just based on a mere Santa Claus test and whether you pass that or fail that, then that alone determines the eternal outcome though it can for some in the case of the doomed. But we will be judged about almost everything in our life in great detail to a greater degree of importance than how I have passed relatively inaccurate neglectful underestimated judgement of the evil of Santa Claus. So just as you now see to some degree, I hope, the great evil that has been done by people supporting Santa Claus, that is just one tiny aspect of life. We have done so many things without realizing the importance of what we have done and how angry we have made our Creator or how pleased we have made our Creator. And that is the scary reality that everyone will face and even though we have been warned to some extent we have not given the proper seriousness to the matter of what we do with our life and time. Neither me, my wife, nor even the prophets, or angels assigned to be in charge of punishing criminals in hellfire have truly appreciated the terror that awaits us all on Judgement Day. For even the angels who may punish us in the Hellfire have yet to realize the extent of the Hellfire's eternal growth in pain levels, nor have the angels in paradise known the extent of the eternal pleasures there and what the inhabitants of each will gain by being in paradise and lose by being in Hell. Only Allah knows the seriousness of how valuable our short life of tiny effort is worth according to divine evaluation and how great an impact every second has. Yet it is a true fact that no matter how religious we may feel or act, we have not done justice with the blessings given to us regarding our usage of them and it is not possible to ever do so. Thus we must just try harder and harder everyday to be better and better in every way in every second we have left. So then maybe out of all the billions of criminals who have not done as good a job as they could have done for all of time, perhaps Allah will make an exceptional excuse for us and mercifully grant us extra blessed guidance that benefits us so we can improve more. This is hoped for so after such merciful blessed improvement aided by Allah then perhaps we may do something that may matter enough in importance to our one and only divine powerful Creator that will qualify us to potentially receive eternal mercy by virtue of doing something right that led us to die in a state where Allah was satisfied enough not to punish us eternally as deserved and reward us eternally as undeserved of it as we are, just to display Allah's mercy and appreciation for goodness that Allah alone facilitates those blessed by Allah to be able to do with pure intentions according to the prophetic method. And if even after all that effort we fail the test of life and burn in hellfire eternally as we might be destined to deserve, then at least we may not have as bad a spot in hell as we would have had we not tried to improve with maximum sincerity and prophetic knowledge-based effort. At the very least we will not have as much regret in hell than we would have had we just kept doing as we had done thus far, or gotten worse as time passes. The point is religion is so much more important than any creature realizes and it encompasses everything.

So when we do meet don't think it is going to be an entirely secular non-religious type of experience as such experiences do not exist in reality. In reality every second of life is recorded and we will be brought to judgement for it. There are no moments of free time that are not given any importance by our Divine Judge. So while everything in life has a religious value, practically life also involves fluctuation of priorities and activities. However me and my wife are not secular people and we do not want to be around secular people who have no interest or time or tolerance for religion and religious benefit in their life. Our life is too valuable to spend time ignoring reality for the sake of experiencing the company of people who will not help us get a higher level in the afterlife and if anything will only make us worse people that involve us in sins. So then we end up disowning each other mutually disgusted on Judgment Day at the time we spent together since neither of us got any eternal goodness from the experience at all.

If you don't like religion being involved in tribal interactions then you don't like me or my wife. But we will not reiterate the definitions of the word "like" and such, as we did with "love". The point that Islam should define me and my wife cannot be ignored. Especially as we are expected to get more Islamic and more religious as we all grow older. So in any future meeting definitely expect there to be an involvement of Islam and religion to some extent, more than I have struggled to introduce in the past tribal meetings. Simply because our love and fear of Allah should grow over time as we come closer to death. So while it is not an easy constant elevator ride up of religiosity and improvement there should be a pattern of increase when measured on a timeline. So be prepared for that if you ever meet us in person. It's probably not going to be as religiously themed of an interaction as our Creator would like because we are weak humans who are flawed. But we should care more about Allah's laws regarding right/wrong than any opinion or number of opinions any tribe members may have. So if you don't like these rules of engagement, we don't care despite our care for you.

We know these rules are not easily practiced in this country and we plan to move to a land where it is easier to live Islamically before having kids if Allah facilitates it. So hopefully Allah makes my time left in America short and we are not around much more to potentially bother you or have you potentially bother us, or either of us fall into sin due to interacting ignorantly, angrily or insincerely. Then hopefully Allah does not prolong our life too long so that we lose strength to be upon goodness. But whether we are in America for a longer than expected time or live a longer than expected time, every day we must get more religious or we will regret it. Thus with this being our belief then if you want to play games with us and just have a "normal interaction" like we did in the past prior to my Islam or even during my Islam in previous experiences then this is something we want to avoid. Such a plot to just shrug it off and maintain the secularist status quo could even be attempted once and even all the rules we mentioned could be disregarded or violated if Allah destines such a disaster to occur. But the prophetic teaching dictates the believers are not stung by the same hole twice. So if you want to play games and disrespect these few highly important rules I have explained which we try hard to live by, then we will not be motivated much to have many more meetings under such circumstances that we deem sinfully unacceptable. We do not want to damage tribal ties by any unnecessary methods but we also highly value having as clear a conscious as possible. As a husband who is not only responsible for my own spiritual safety but my wife's as well and any future children we have to live according to our true beliefs upon the prophetic faith. So things Islam deems sinful that I may have bitterly regretfully tolerated being done around me in the past without much objection or comment about, despite my heart's pain and frustration, cannot be repeated again. And I want to make such repeat moments of sin and regret extremely unlikely to ever occur again by taking all possible precautions I can to protect myself and my wife from a blazing fire with no end.

As I bring this letter to an eventual end the situation of our Islam and lack of proper assessment of our tribe's religious differences according to sincere knowledgeable analysis, truth seeking and virtue building remains to be concluded. Me and my wife are fundamentally seeking a guarantee of safety to practice Salafi Islam amongst you if we ever meet together in person without us falling into the sins previously mentioned in these pages. I understand how surprising and seemingly difficult and crazy the situation we find ourselves and yourselves in is. I am not unaware of what I have done and what I am praying is achieved in the short or long run, if Allah makes it happen. I know exactly what I sound like. The main goal is not readers, or responses, or correct reactions. The goal should be to fulfill a sacred religious obligation to invite the members of my tribe to goodness as the prophets taught us to do as they were commanded by the

Creator to do under threat of eternal punishment for not doing so. Despite a shared faith and understanding my wife is more compassionate to you than I am, perhaps because she doesn't know you as well as I do, or have as strong of an emotional concern over you burning in hellfire for eternity if you die upon other than Islam, or perhaps because she is not as responsible for teaching you your errors and fixing them because I have a closer bond to you than her. My wife herself based on her knowledge of me and lack of knowledge of you even advised me against such blessed invitations, at least at this time. Yet when it comes to obeying our Creator, we don't have options to choose the best time because time is something we cannot control, nor know in advance. So truly there may not be another time for me, or for some of you. Despite the likelihood of such a message never being read, what needs to be said needs to be said even if the message remains unknown and unheard and unpopular and unwanted and unappreciated by creatures. Because it is not done for your benefit, nor my wife's benefit, nor for my benefit. All deeds should only be done for the sake of the Creator of life so that when our life ends it was a life worth something to its Creator and because of that it is treasured by its Maker, instead of a negative defective invention that does not fulfill the purpose for which it was designed and instructed and empowered to accomplish. Even while knowing how unlikely a positive reaction to my Islamic invitation and warning may seem, still despite the calculations and negative forecasts indicating little statistical chance of any remote type of religious improvement in the situation, which may even get worse as a result, I will invite you to the truth of Salafi Islam and request you join us in religious improvement upon the prophetic faith.

I admit and regret my failures as a tribe member, which you may recognize or not, in the past both as a non-Muslim and even as a Muslim. Additionally, I apologize in advance for those failures that are likely to occur in the future imperfections of the course of our human existence. These failures have not helped my credibility levels or status in your estimation to make my advice more appreciated or desirable. I truly was the worst person in our tribe for years prior to Islam whether you know it or not.

This is because I was the most anti-Islamic of all of us, I was the most pro-Christian of all of us promoting the polytheistic anthropomorphic shirk of Trinitarian sonhood/ghosthood, crucifixion/communion mythology. I was so pro-Christian that even with most of you being Christians some of you even felt intimidated by my Christian zeal and fervor, which I expanded upon as I grew training to become a professional priest, celibate for life for the sake of my misunderstanding of God. And even that wasn't Christian enough to satisfy my missionary goals to convert the world to worshipping Jesus and the mythical "one and only holy bible inspired by the holy ghost to several holy characters translated by unknown holy men passed down to us to inform us of the holy prophet who died on a holy cross to give us a holy piece of bread and holy drink of wine which fills us with a ghost making us semi-divine". And I would even pass out this same food and drink in the churches during worship services uttering blasphemy I cannot repeat today, doing so at a record-young teenage age. Still I did more, teaching dozens of 3rd graders and 5th graders Christian religion classes weekly for several years to nurture their beliefs of falsehood.

Yet still I went even further into error making Christian music to advance the cause you witnessed me grow up upon and be willing to sacrifice my sex life and my real life for. Yet even more I would attend Church services daily, despite being a full-time college student saying the innovative rosary bead prayers daily as well. Had I died upon such beliefs and activities I assure you I would have eternally burned suffering in hell forever in misery. Most of you have done much less for the Christian cause or the war against Islam than I have. So you have less skin in the game for the sake of Satan so the pain should be much less when crying over the regret of acknowledged religious errors and the joy will be much greater when accepting the truth because you have done so much less Anti-Islamic evil in the world than I have. I may inevitably offend you by citing your sinful errors making you feel guilt or anger or embarrassment because of them, but as bad as Christianity and any faith other than Islam is, I don't imagine any of you can ever get to be as much of an enemy of the prophetic Islam as I was. Thus whatever regret for sins you can ever feel, when I have done so many more sins of greater magnitude than you in a much shorter timeframe as a Kafir fighting Islam intentionally with a heart waging war against Islam just because it wasn't Christianity then that makes me most likely the person with the biggest anti-Islamic criminal record in our tribe, who is still alive. Hence I was the worst of us according to Islamic standards. If you think otherwise and instead say that I wasn't that bad then but now because of Islam and trying to be Muslim, then now I am truly the worst of all our tribe then please bring me the proof for this idea so I can improve. For there are two fundamental solutions for all unbalanced religious errors. 1. Sincerity and 2. Knowledge. When ignorance or stupidity or confusion for whatever reason is the problem then the religious issues can be fixed over time and heal with medicinal prophetic knowledge as given to our species by its Creator. However if the problem is sincerity, it is a much bigger problem. This is because insincerity makes prophetic knowledge, warnings and advice to be of no benefit. As Satan our enemy has 100% knowledge of all the prophetic knowledge with absolutely correct belief and accuracy regarding who taught what, when, why, where and how. Satan believes in everything correctly and even has more knowledge about our Creator who created him than all the prophets combined together since he even existed before humans did. Satan's problem is his insincerity, not his lack of prophetic knowledge/data. So what is my problem? And what is your problem? Who is lacking religious knowledge of the prophetic faith? Who is lacking sincerity which cannot be taught, or bought, or grown, or traded for, or acquired by any means unless the Creator of your soul blesses you with it? But even then if given Sincerity, it doesn't seal the salvation of the soul because the prophetic knowledge guides the sincerity to act correctly so stupidity and ignorance or emotions don't cause the sincere person to sin and mistakenly go to hell by accident expecting something else.

Your transition to Islam would likely not be as hard as mine and you wouldn't be alone either, nor the first to rattle the tribe's prison cage of disbelief. Do you care more about unislamic religions than I did? Then if you "loved us" you would defend them and bring us better guidance to act more righteous. Frighteningly the possibilities are vanishing and suspected deficiencies are becoming obvious. Yet anyone can change any minute with Allah's blessing. Perhaps you fear sadness due to difficult religious development? On the contrary true happiness is one of lawful slave-like obedience to the Master of all things. Happiness and Sadness is always in the control of the Creator. And the cursed life is the one spent chasing happiness in other endeavors. During the timeline of your lifetime, I vow you have not yet tasted happiness once. For me making one Salat to Allah is worth much more than every pleasure our whole tribe wants. You cannot lose by stopping any sin the Creator of happiness forbade despite what statistics may seem to indicate. So don't be scared or fearful of losing what miserable emotions you call happiness today, and thereby delay doing the right things making you suffer hellfire eternally.

My medical providers routinely test my cognitive abilities and my mentality checking for impairment or retardation or stupidity or loss of brain function or craziness. If you wish I can have my doctor and therapist write you official medical notes testifying that I am not stupid or crazy or whatever else you may think is a possible reason for why I would be

Muslim and insist you become Muslim practicing Islam too. So if it is medically proven that I am not stupid or crazy then what is it? Why would one of the shyest relatives in our tribe, with the least social experience out of anyone else, due to being the only only child in the family, voluntarily choose to risk all the easily avoidable and predictable explosions of anger/gossip/trouble/insults/stress/hurt feelings of the tribe by changing their traditional tribal friendly faith and then inviting you all to do so as well? Do you think I have no factual evidence that proves the claims I make? Do you think I am totally unaware of your own religions and their creeds and practices, so that I cannot correctly compare religions reasonably with studious scholastic responsibility? Do you know me to joke around when it comes to religion and not view religion as something important? If I am so wrong then why would you let your beloved go to eternal hell if you know better? Correct me if I am wrong on anything, please! Does writing this and sending this letter make my life easier? Truly I feel it is a much easier process for me to experience being wrong and get corrected than it is for me to correct you when you are wrong. So it makes my life a lot easier if I am wrong regarding religion and need to change to improve because I am better able to fix myself who I have some control over, than you who I have so little influence over despite our tribal connection. Or do you think I know I am wrong and intentionally lying to you as part of a sinister evil plot to take myself to the deepest depths of eternal hell and drag you into it with me? Have I not been transparent and fair in my advice to you? Or do you feel I am hiding secret wicked motives?

Are my words the words of liars? Are yours?

Are my words the words of idiots? Are yours?

Are my words the words of crazies? Are yours?

Are my words the words of jokers? Are yours?

Are my words the words of speculators? Are yours?

Are my words the words of the ill-informed? Are yours?

Are my words the words of devils? Are yours?

Or are all these words the words which Allah our Creator is aware of in full detail which I am

communicating to you? Are these not words which
our Creator is causing you to be exposed to, or is
causing you to suffer the lost opportunity of
missing out on good advice? Of which the outcome
for the recipients of these words differs depending
on the destiny our Creator has decided is best for
those blessed to be blessed and those cursed to be
cursed. So when our Creator later asks you about
whether you reacted correctly and sincerely to your
long letter from your "beloved" tribal Muslim when
they were inviting you to goodness, what will you
say? There is no escape from the blessed destined
invitations or challenges of Allah. Allah alone
caused me to live amongst you, be related to you,
and allowed me to try teaching you about prophetic
Islam. So what alternative solution, if any, do you
propose to me to get the family to unite upon
proven true pure prophetic religion so all of us can
be blessed and go to paradise with nobody amongst
us going to Hell if Allah grants such a blessing?
You can delay a correct religious reaction in disgust
and secret or publicized hatred awaiting my future
death as all creatures wait for death, which they
cannot avoid. But you will have a much easier
conversation with me regarding religion than you

will with the Angel of Death who already has you on his list of appointments. If Allah wills my religious intensity for our mutual goodness will increase overall as I age and we all have less time left to solve the devilish tribal division regarding doctrines and deeds. So I suggest making some big religious lifelong efforts, in the prophetic direction of goodness, because the family dynamic has changed. Islam is here in our universe and grows as Allah decrees regardless of who loves it, likes it, dislikes it, hates it, fights for it or fights against it, intentionally or unintentionally, regardless of what anyone of us does about it. Our impact for or against Islam is not noticeable, but Allah's impact of Islam on us is the only thing that matters. Lastly for those who prefer hypothetical game playing when it comes to their faith: If Islam is true as I so strongly confidently offer to prove to you, and then you react to this Islamic warning and invitation as you do, will you be eternally happy fully satisfied 100% with your actions and have no regrets?

Or shall you be upset that your own tribal member came to you with this great opportunity before Divine Judgement?

You are left with no excuse for any of you to deny for even the blink of an eye. The absolutely terrifying truth that I testify to you now, though not knowing or rather believing it myself when I was among you as a youth. That the Arabic Quran is uncreated speech it is not the words of any human or even possibly written by the special blessed ones sent as Prophets. The Arabic Quran is uncreated speech it is not the words of any Jinn. The devils cannot battle it when it is believed in with true conviction instead of mere lipservice and Tajweed recitation. Iblis or Satan has no weapon to use against Allah's light. All devils of humans and jinn feel the Quran's divine might, no matter whether they flee from it or try to fight. The Arabic Quran cannot be magic or the words of the insane. Nor is the Arabic Quran angelic despite all angels always praising Allah's name. So willingly or unwillingly all creatures will come to know. The Arabic Quran sent by Allah will set the standard you must follow. Or go to Hell forever and lie to yourselves some more. Since the more each creature sins and errs the more they forget what they are made for. So few have passed the test and I have no guarantee. Be glad for the test you have and that it is not one of greater difficulty. For prophets had much greater proof and had to teach obligatorily. The prophets had no unislamic options to choose, and neither do any of you. Muslims themselves can do nothing, nor is it legal for me to make threats. Yet death is your known promise and guaranteed destiny you try to forget. Many say they are ready to die never to do another deed, and think their Maker is pleased and entry to Paradise is a formality. Yet what evidence do they have when they mention some deity they haven't seen? Allah has yet to reveal many details but his power is beyond all of all creation's dreams. So choose the winning team or scream in eternal pain. For Salafiyyah as Muhammad taught it is the only available form of safety. Had you not been tribe members or perhaps if my wife were here, we would do the obligatory duty challenging all of you to truly beg our Creator to curse the one who lies! Why does that frighten anyone? Did Allah not already promise that such was done? So if I challenge you aloud, or in writing, what difference would my words make? I have no abilities whatsoever to Give or Take away any amount of Faith. My own faith is not my possession to even imagine it as something great. It

is only ignorance and sinful insincerity that causes
lack of faith. Of which ignorance is always an
attribute of any created being Allah ever creates. So
whether anyone curses invoking Allah or they
don't, whether they are truthful or lie, no amount of
debating or challenges will benefit those destined to
die, inside their very soul which they hide from
themselves so much they are surprised. The one
who created them will be the one to criticize. I'm
just trying to finish a mission before Allah makes
me die, in what way I do not know, nor do I know
how many times. Yet I testify nobody is ready even
those the prophets promised Paradise. For all you
got left is one Divine book with a Sunnah to guide
the lives. The Straight Path of the elite blessed
slaves will continue to survive, you will not; and
time expires before we are properly terrorized.
Truly all lives are worthless except those whom
Allah declares as prized. And until you die and go,
and later rise with dripping tearful eyes to know
your full account with the Judge most Wise with all
the clout, you will forever lack understanding of
what life is always about. Why have you slept
nights you should have wept for steps you took to
sin with ever increasingly wicked grins? How long

will you deny? Who among you has tried to cry?
Who among you has thought of suicide inside?
How many signs will you criticize? Please pick
your prize before your demise! Why do you lie in
pride when you are famous for shameful sins? For
your time is nearly over and ignoring Islam is
impossible. For the true Divine faith cannot be
stopped and those who try will suffer misanthropic
torture indescribable. For too long you have
avoided the important life purpose of worship. So
wait upon your warship as the floods of the
inevitable reality comes to collect you. There may
not be many moments of decision-making left in
life. At least don't cause strife for me and my wife
when you know inside your soul that the faith on
your side isn't right.

Finally as a warning to those who value books or
writing, and think this must be good because of the
hearts with locks which it might've shook. Allah
will question everyone and that only happens to the
blessed ones. The cursed ones get a similar
response as they gave to Allah when Allah destined
someone amongst them invite them, eternal
ignoring no matter how painful their cries begging

for dialog may sound. I am no Messenger of Allah as Muhammad is the last one. Allah made the perfect selection choosing the best created character for us to learn from. What more can be said to start the conversation that leads to speaking with Allah in private after death, one-on-one; without any translation or misinterpretation? Which one will you die being, one of the blessed or one of the cursed? Has your heart become sub-human filled with venom from self-inflicted pollution and the mind molten lava from brainwashing? Or has your soul just been waiting for someone or something to remind it? What preparation have you made for death? To what and who have you paid attention? What more in the form of an advisory warning for your own soul's benefit must a Muslim mention?

Quran 42:19-25

"Allâh is very Gracious and Kind to His slaves. He gives provisions to whom He wills. And He is the All-Strong, the All-Mighty. Whosoever desires (by his deeds) the reward of the Hereafter, We give him increase in his reward, and whosoever desires the reward of this world (by his deeds), We give him thereof (what is decreed for him), and he has no portion in the Hereafter.

Or have they partners [other deities] who have ordained for them a religion to which Allāh has not consented? But if not for the decisive word, it would have been concluded between them. And indeed, the wrongdoers will have a painful punishment. You will see the wrongdoers fearful of what they have earned, and it will [certainly] befall them. And those who have believed and done righteous deeds will be in lush regions of the gardens [in Paradise] having whatever they will in the presence of their Lord. That is what is the great bounty. That is (the Paradise) whereof Allâh gives glad tidings to His slaves who believe (in the Oneness of Allâh - Islâmic Monotheism) and do righteous good deeds. Say: "No reward do I ask of you for this except to be kind to me for my kinship with you." And whoever earns a good righteous deed, We shall give him an increase of good in respect thereof. Verily, Allâh is Oft-Forgiving, Most Ready to appreciate (the deeds of those who are obedient to Him). Or do they say, "He has invented about Allāh a lie"? But if Allāh willed, He could seal over your heart. And Allāh eliminates falsehood and establishes the truth by His words. Indeed, He is Knowing of that within the hearts. And He it is Who accepts repentance from His slaves, and forgives sins, and He knows what you do."

Quran 66:6-7

O you who have believed, protect yourselves and your families from a Fire whose fuel is people and stones, over which are angels, harsh and severe; they do not disobey Allāh in what He commands them but do what they are commanded. O you who have disbelieved, make no excuses that Day. You will only be recompensed for what you used to do.

Quran 103

By time, Indeed, mankind is in loss, Except for those who have believed and done righteous deeds and advised each other to truth and advised each other to patience.

Abu Huraira reported: *A man said to the Messenger of Allah, "I have relatives with whom I try to maintain good relationship but they sever relations with me; whom I treat kindly but they treat me badly, with whom I am gentle but they are rough to me." He replied, "If you are as you have said, then it is as though you are feeding them hot ashes and you will not be without a supporter against them from Allah, as long as you do so".*

Source: Ṣaḥīḥ Muslim 2558

Abu Huraira said: the Messenger of Allah said,

"By the One in whose hand is the soul of Muhammad, none from this nation of Jews and Christians hears of me, and then dies without having faith in my message, but that he will be an inhabitant of Hellfire."

Source: Sahih Muslim 153

NO PAGE IN YOUR BOOK OF DEEDS ON THE DAY OF TERROR SHOULD BE BLANK OR WASTED WITH SINS EVEN IF IT IS ERASED BY ALLAH DUE TO REPENTANCE.

www.ingramcontent.com/pod-product-compliance
Lightning Source LLC
Chambersburg PA
CBHW071220130726
47998CB00002B/793